NOW *Get Up* AND GO BE GREAT!

JENNIFER BISHOP

Printed in the United States of America
First Printing, 2020
Empowered to Prosper LLC.
Empowered to Prosper-Publishing
ISBN:978-1-7350681-0-7
www.bishopspeaks.com

DEDICATION

This book is dedicated to the Essential Workers and First Responders who gave themselves so selflessly during the COVID-19 pandemic of 2020.

And to my very first, First Responder, my Momma. Every breath you breathed filled my lungs. I will make sure to live for both of us now. I love you.

CONTENTS

CONFIDENCE 9
CONQUEROR 15
ENCOURAGEMENT 21
ENDURANCE 29
PEACE 35
LIFE 43
RELENTLESS 51
STRENGTH 59
WISDOM 65

A Letter from Me to You

I reflected upon a quote from author Idowu Koyenikan, "Acquiring wisdom is great, but it is not the goal, applying it is.". In reflecting on that quote, I realized that I wanted to give you a suggested strategy to engage this book.

As you read *Now Get Up and Go Be Great*, consider the following steps to make this journey impactful:

Step 1:

Identify a Relatable Thought

Step 2:

Reflect on the Meaning of the Thought

Step 3:

Personalize the Thought

Step 4:

Share the Thought

I am excited for you. I believe that you are investing in yourself by reading this book. More importantly, when you share this book, you will be investing in others.

Now get up and go be great!

QR Code

You are embarking on an essential journey with this book. One thing that I have learned about being on that journey of self-discovery and re-discovery is that there will be times when you need to talk. To be motivated or just to know that you are not alone. For that very reason, I have created a platform to engage in the journey. You can share with others how you are doing or how this tool helps you get up and be great.

Will you join us?

ACKNOWLEDGEMENTS

Bishop, you are the love of my life. Your love, strength, and unwavering belief in my capacity and your inspiration helped me to fly; I love you.

Peyton, you are my reason to push beyond limits. I am humbled that God entrusted me with you. I will forever move mountains to protect you and preserve you.

Daddy, you are a man of kindness, peace, consistency, and responsibility. I love you more than you will ever know.

Auntie Cyde, you are my angel on this earth. You have been my Lifeguard, and your love not only helped to raise me but it also helped to save me. I am eternally grateful.

To my siblings Kristen, Kelly, and Henry, God knew what I needed when He allowed us to combine forces. I love you.

To the Bishop Family, there are no in-laws or out-laws with us; there is only family. Thank you for loving me.

To my Grace Christian Church Family, your love is enduring and pure, and for that, I am thankful.

To My Crew, we will forever be by each other's side for whatever and whenever.

To my family that watches me from Heaven, especially my sweet baby girl Erin, I love you, and one day, we will meet again.

And to my God, thank you for keeping me. This life has brought joys and pains, and yet without each experience, this book would not have come into existence. I needed them all.

CONFIDENCE

The songwriter John P. Kee wrote these lyrics in the song *You Don't Know My Story*, "You don't know my story, you don't know the things that I've come through, you cannot imagine, the pain, the trials I've had to endure." Such powerful words. People don't know how you have made it this far, and here are the significant facts, you are still standing! You are powerful! You are ready, and you should have the confidence that your survival dictates you deserve to have. I want you to find that version of yourself that allows you to move in a sphere of freedom and confidence to be who you are and never let that person go. Now get up and go be great!

The distance between your dreams and reality is a verb called action.

Truth is the truth! It will work anywhere!

Today, think about all that you are instead of all that you think you are not!

Don't ever confuse education with intelligence. There are many idiots with degrees.

Deep down, you already know the truth.

Now and then, you have to slide your credentials across the table so that they know it is not a game.

The cloth I'm cut from is permanently sold out.

If you were arrested for being a Christian, would there be enough evidence to convict you?

Never fear the strongest. Fear the one that never gives up.

There are two sides to every story; then there are the screenshots.

They may try to steal your recipe, but the sauce won't taste the same.

I can show you my hand, and I will still win.

All of the looking back you are doing will put a crook in your neck.

Never dumb it down. Make them come up and get it.

The Lord sent me here to live an extraordinary life. Kindly avoid me if mediocrity is your calling.

When they start to move funny, you need to move right out of the way.

Sometimes you will need to deal with people how they deal with you; barely, hardly, and accordingly.

Stop making what someone did to you more significant than what God did for you.

Why do you keep trying to retain what God has told you to release?

The only thing they can take from you is notes.

Being okay if it works out and being okay if it does not work out is a powerful place.

Part of meeting people where they are is also knowing when to leave them there.

I would much rather inspire than impress.

Perhaps your heart hurts because you have focused more on speaking passively rather than speaking truthfully.

CONQUEROR

I am a manifestation of all of the things I have survived. I am still here, the good, the bad, and the excruciating. Standing tall and accelerating forward through all of the situations, I thought I would not survive. I am a conqueror, and so are you. Now get up and go be great!

So many people know the solution because they caused the problem.

They thought it would break you when it really built you.

Be careful of the people who have access to you. You can't make good decisions with bad information.

Sometimes it will take a lot to realize what you are unwilling to take.

It's your time to shine. Don't dim your light.

Welcome to the season where people are going to regret betting against you.

They ask, "How are y'all striving?" We told them, "We conquered just surviving."

Don't let anyone take you back to a level you graduated from.

There is something special about a woman who overcomes everything sent to destroy her.

Life doesn't come with a spare.

Many people want to be counted in but can't be counted on.

Marriages will have a higher survival rate when spouses start using game plans instead of attack plans.

Before you test deep waters, make sure that you can swim.

If you are irritated by every rub, how will you ever get polished?

People get really mad that they left you to die, and you didn't.

Not everyone staring at you is admiring you. Some are amazed that you survived the traps that they set for you.

Remember when the devil won? Neither do I!

People don't abandon people they care about. They abandon the people they were using. Know the difference.

Whether in your vehicle or your relationship, learn the difference between the riders and the hitchhikers.

You can't stop the waves, but you can learn how to surf.

There is no need to respond immediately to everything you hear or see but believe that you should bookmark that bad boy for later.

Be careful of the beast that you let out. Some of them don't go back into their cages.

Let go of it or be dragged by it.

Don't drown trying to be everyone else's anchor.

If people know your name, they should know it for a reason.

ENCOURAGEMENT

There is a video clip of a UCLA basketball player walking down the court with his head hung low, trying to process the gravity of a significant mistake made during the game. As he walks down the court, his teammate runs up behind him, daps him up, lifts his chin, pats him on the back, and heads off in another direction to get ready for the next play. In that moment of encouragement, you can instantly see how the transfer of empowerment changed the course of the rest of his game. That video empowers and encourages me every time I see or think of it. There is a real underestimation of the power of enabling another person and even encouraging ourselves. So, don't forget, a pat on someone's back can cause their chin to lift and their shoulders to set back so that they can go on to play the rest of the game. Now get up and go be great!

Be clear; God is perfect. You are not.

Stop replacing substance with sizzle.

Stop trusting what is not trustworthy.

Introspection brings about your facts and your truths. They each will stare you in the face and dare you to blink. We call this facing it to fix it. Try it.

Stop giving do-overs to people who treat you like leftovers!

If they aren't proud of you, then they aren't for you.

Peep it. Adjust it. Move on.

You have survived so much. Why are you still letting people waste your time?

People only show you their picture. They don't show you the process.

You are too powerful to play it safe.

The very people who did you wrong will be the same ones who have to watch God do you right.

Stop pressing rewind, and just hit delete.

Realize that you can lose your mind waiting on them to make up theirs.

You can't ride for someone who keeps jumping in and out of the car.

Always keep your face towards the sunshine, and the shadows will always be behind you.

Sometimes you will not know the value of a moment until it becomes a memory.

Your ministry is found where you have been broken. Your testimony is found where you have been restored.

Funny how they talk about who fell off when they have never been on.

Today is a new day. Stay controlled and stay focused. What you can't control and what you can't manage is not yours to touch. It belongs to God.

Speaking out isn't easy. It's okay not to be okay.

When you doubt your power, you give power to your doubt.

Jealousy is a disease. Pray they get better soon.

I laugh when people try to figure me out. I'm still figuring myself out.

Your vision will be clearer when you get more focused.

Don't stop imagining what you want until you start managing what you wanted.

You inspire people who pretend not to even see you. Trust me.

If you have to search for a reason to stay, realize that you have already found a reason to leave.

Chase your dreams, not people.

The same ones that say that you can't are the same ones that are afraid that you will.

If someone else talked to you how you talk to you, you would be ready to fight. Stop it.

God isn't letting you down. He is letting you learn.

Baby, you can be the entire package and still end up at the wrong address.

How your life feels is more important than how your life looks.

You need you.

ENDURANCE

We have all had to endure unspeakable trials and unfathomable tribulations in this life. Endurance doesn't just prove that you can withstand the winds of circumstance and the blows of the battle. Endurance demonstrates that you can recover and rejoice. You were built for this, no matter what comes your way. Now get up and go be great!

Failure is a bruise, not a tattoo, and falling is not the problem. Staying down is.

Self-doubt is and enemy. Kill it.

I'm not racing with the person beside me. I'm racing with the person inside me.

I thought about quitting; then I noticed who was watching me.

There is no miracle in the familiar.

Maybe your journey isn't about moving forward. Perhaps it is about moving back to who you were created to be.

It is incredible how bright your future looks when you can see God's promises instead of your problems.

Success will ask you one question, "How bad do you want it?"

They better either grow with you, or you better outgrow them. Do not stand still for anybody!

If we don't climb the mountain, we will never see the view.

Be so loud that they can't ignore you.

The first step of change is becoming aware of your own crap.

When God opens the next door, you will see why the enemy fought you so hard.

The wait wasn't punishment. It was preparation.

Don't displace what you can't replace.

Experience has taught me to stop praying for lighter burdens and pray for a stronger back.

Setback time is over. Comeback time is here.

It is not always the words that hurt you. Most of the time, it is the person who said them to you that did.

Nothing profound about it. Nothing prolific with it. Just make up your mind and do it.

The most important lesson I have learned was not to stress the should haves and could haves because if it were meant to be, it would have.

Do you want to know why you keep getting reality checks? Because you keep depositing excuses.

My life took shape when I realized I could no longer conform.

Don't let anyone tell you that your intuitions are your insecurities.

PEACE

Do you know what sweet peace is? Have you found your peace yet? Have you seen the place in your space on this earth where no matter where you are, and no matter what is going on around you, there is still a sweet peace that truly surpasses all understanding? It took me a long time to find a place where my peace was my priority. And now that I have safely arrived at this place of peace, I have unpacked, and I am not moving. And my friend, I am here to tell you that you will do the same thing when you find your peace. Now get up and go be great!

Always remember that you can sleep tight at night when you are right.

Your competition isn't other people. It's your procrastination. Your ego. The knowledge you neglect. The negative behavior you are nurturing. If you want to compete, compete against that.

When did being right become more important than doing right?

If you aren't scared, you aren't living.

They think that you came up. You know that God came through.

Yes, you can be an intellectual and ratchet at the same time. It is called balance. Embrace it!

Don't tell me what they said about me if I can't reference you when I address them.

Beautiful is the soul who is in alignment with its divine purpose!

Too many people are trying to find peace through a pill.

If it doesn't bring me peace or make me happy, I can't afford it. My energy is on a strict budget, and my Platinum "Not Dealing with Crap" AMEX card will decline all pettiness, trivialness, and mess on site. Check your credit and see if you can get approved for one of those cards.

Believe you deserve it, and God will serve it!

Stop posting about what you need to pray about!

Freedom is when you finally realize that their ceiling is your floor.

Stop feeding people who just want a plate to go.

Each day I understand the phrase "I'm getting too old for this" on a deeper level.

Whatever you lost wasn't yours.

When you are in a position of peace, you are in a position of power.

I don't hold grudges. I remember the facts.

Stop comparing your life to someone else's social media page. Their page is staged.

There are times when my greatest accomplishment is just keeping my mouth shut.

If you are tired of the drama in your life, stop being the lead actor.

If it doesn't make me happy or make me money at this stage of life, I don't have time for it.

You will lose yourself trying to hold on to someone who doesn't care about losing you.

There will be times when silence is a perfect answer.

I need to teach my facial expressions to use their inside voice.

One day you will learn to choose happiness over history.

Stop disturbing their peace because you are at war with yourself.

When the chemistry is gone, history doesn't matter.

They say you are holding grudges. Nah, you are maintaining boundaries.

There will be times when the unanswered prayer is the answered prayer.

If it will cost you your peace, it is too expensive.

Peace is often found at the intersection of pain and promise.

Inner peace does not come cheap. You will pay a heavy price.

LIFE

Things have happened and will happen to you that you cannot control and that most times you will not understand. Whether in your relationships, in your finances, with your faith, or on your job, you can handle it. Control the controllable and manage the manageable. Everything else belongs to God. Now get up and go be great!

When you throw dirt, you lose ground. Stop hating and start participating.

Your problem is not in your eyes. It's in your environment.

I refuse to live as half of me because people can't handle all of me.

Why are you waiting to be invited to their party when you are supposed to be throwing your own?

If they won't stand up, then tell them to stand back.

I'm a real fan of watching people grow to become a happier and healthier version of themselves. You are growing, and it is showing.

If you don't love yourself, you'll always be chasing after people who don't love you either. Stop chasing them and start chasing you.

Yes, you should be forgiving. Yes, you should be understanding. No, you should not be a fool.

I cut myself off in the middle of a bad thought and say, "Girl, we don't have time for this." You should do the same.

Know your worth, then add federal, state, local taxes, shipping, handling, cancellation, and processing fees.

Learn to love the sound of your feet walking away from things that are not meant for you.

Some so many people love you. Stop focusing on the ones that don't.

God is not punishing you; He is preparing you. Trust His plan, not your pain.

Love yourself first because that is who you will be spending the rest of your life with.

Many people spend too much time trying to find someone to sleep with instead of finding someone worth waking up to.

You didn't lose him. You found you.

The moment that you start to contemplate if you deserve better, you do.

Know that God isn't trying to inflict you with pain; He is trying to infuse you with your promise.

Courage isn't that you aren't afraid. Courage is knowing that you are afraid and moving forward anyway.

Happiness is a state of mind. What state do you live in?

I will fight for you; however, I will not compete for you. There is a difference.

You are allowed to be both a masterpiece and a work in progress at the same time.

Be clear. What is for you won't be toxic to you.

Instead of getting even with those that hurt you, try getting even with those that helped you.

God has a habit of picking nobodies and turning them into somebodies without consulting anybody.

It is hilarious how so many people have the answers to other people's problems.

Stop being afraid of helping other people get on. If you are good at what you do, your spot isn't up for grabs.

Do you want to learn how to exercise? Start with learning how to exercise discretion.

Get out of the season of throwing hints and hoping that people catch them. Say what needs to be said.

Stop looking at the situation as if you were being rejected. You were being rescued.

You need you way more than you will ever need them. Trust me on this one.

Sometimes you have to start showing people just how important they aren't.

RELENTLESS

I watched the Michael Jordan documentary, The Last Dance, and sat in awe at his tenacity, his passion, and his relentlessness for not just the game of basketball but his gift. I looked at the documentary in veneration, not only because I witnessed the behind-the-scenes of his journey but because I recognized it. I, too, have that relentless passion, and my game-changer was learning to respect it and then tap into it. When you do, the only force that can stop a relentless pursuit of your passion is you. Now get up and go be great!

Be careful of the people who can pinpoint everything wrong about you, yet when it's your turn to point, their pen doesn't seem to want to work.

When someone says you can't do it, do it twice and take pictures.

Why do you keep asking people to give you directions to a place they have never been? This is your journey, not theirs.

I grind for two reasons: To better my future and stunt on my past.

I heard the best things in life are free, but I learned that it cost to be the boss.

If Blockbuster hadn't gotten so comfortable, Netflix wouldn't have existed. Let that sink in.

I am not made for everybody. However, I am built for whatever.

They are not mad at you. They are mad it is you!

Stop saying "I'm grown" and be grown!

Some will say, "Don't bite off more than you can chew." I would rather choke on greatness than nibble on mediocrity.

Being hungry isn't enough. You've got to be starving for it.

Learn to let the pain go, or you will quickly realize that you will be dragged by it.

And one day, just like that, you'll rediscover your light. You'll embrace your inner warrior. You'll snatch your power back. And the whole game will change.

Stop shrinking to fit into places that you have outgrown.

You are worried about them matching your fly, but can they match your mental?

Control the controllable and manage the manageable.

Don't play with me because you aren't going to like how I play back.

Perhaps your heart hurts because you have focused more on speaking passively rather than speaking truthfully.

Never let your moment of weakness make you believe that you lack strength.

Don't do something permanently stupid just because you're temporarily upset.

Stop being intimidated by your potential.

Stop giving CPR to dead situations and start pulling plugs.

The moment you are ready to pursue your dreams is when you learn that fear is not a factor.

Why are you expecting unconditional love yet carrying a bag full of conditions?

Loyalty is priceless. Don't waste it on people who take you for granted.

Stop adapting to it and start influencing it.

It is simply amazing how someone can pray on Sunday and then prey on people for the rest of the week.

You do not need a piece of a man; you need peace of mind.

If you are worried about poor preaching in the church's pulpit, it may be because there is poor praying in the pews.

Learn to differentiate between the sound of your intuition guiding you and your traumas misleading you.

The truth may hurt you, but a lie could kill you.

STRENGTH

The most critical test of strength is handling someone who tries to mishandle you. Real strength is when you can look at that person and smile because inside, you are saying, "I am controlling me so that I won't hurt you." Now get up and go be great!

Don't dilute your strength because they can't handle you straight up.

My idea of success is not competing. I don't compete. I eat.

Stop spending the night with someone you can't spend the day with.

Sometimes the new you will have to put the old you in check.

To not be insulted by a person talking, you must first respect the person who is talking. If you don't respect them, then reject them.

There is a fine line between genius and crazy. I like to use that line like a jump rope.

You will not always be motivated, so you have to learn to be disciplined.

My Secret: Keep my mouth shut and work in silence. They will know about it soon.

It is fascinating what you can do when you get away from people with no idea what they are doing.

You were born a female. Life will make you a woman.

A strong woman is one that can smile in the morning as if she wasn't just crying last night.

Today's pain will be tomorrow's strength.

You can't fathom how to change the problem because you can't fathom that you are the problem.

Some of us want a piece of the pie, and some want the recipe.

Pretty words aren't always true, and true words aren't always pretty.

It isn't that it got so much easier. It is that you got so much better.

Stop venting and start praying. You don't need sympathy; you need strength.

They are mad because you were praying while they were playing.

If my strength intimidates you, understand that is your weakness, not mine.

If you always have to be the bigger person, you may need to stop being around such little people.

You are so much stronger than the thoughts that try to steal your strength.

Replacing, "Why is this happening to me?" with "What is this trying to tell me?" has been a game-changer for me.

Life can be a challenging test. Realize that everyone has different questions on their test, so copying someone else won't be the answer.

Just because they desire you does not mean they value you.

WISDOM

Often, the understanding of one with wisdom is confused with knowledge. Knowledge is knowing a fact. Wisdom knows what to do with that fact. Now get up and go be great!

**Satan doesn't attack his allies.
Let that sink in.**

**The direction is so much more
important than speed.
Remember that.**

**Some people you learn from,
some people you grow from,
and some people you just need
to get away from.**

**You can attend church
regularly, but are you attending
church religiously? There is a
difference.**

**My definition came from not
allowing others to define me.**

Don't be amazed by the picture you see. Be amazed by the process the person in the picture has endured to get to the place of peace they can show you in the picture.

Stop walking around with a bad temper, smart mouth, and soft feelings. They don't match.

Remember, every confidant is not confidential.

Be ready. God's timing maybe sooner than you think.

In this life, all you have is your name. Either your name will ring bells or set off alarms.

People will beg for your time then completely waste it.

Darling, you can't date him and raise him.

You will cut off many meaningless people when you stop using gossip as a bonding tool.

To be wise enough to speak today, I had to be humble enough to listen in my yesterday.

Crossing the street without looking both ways is safer than crossing me.

Always remember that I never forget.

Understand that people rock with you for two reasons; either you are official or beneficial.

Why are you having relationship problems with someone you are not in a relationship with?

You will forget the pain when you see the payoff.

The problem is that we keep running back to the very place that made us start running in the first place.

Stop airing people's dirty laundry like your laundry has been cleaned.

Give them too much too often, and they forget that you are a privilege.

Sometimes it's the ones you look out for that you need to look out for.

Confidence will always scare the weak.

At this stage in life, you don't need opinions. You need wise counsel.

You haven't found perfection in yourself, so stop expecting it from other people.

Be teachable. You are not always right.

Baby girl, you have already proven that you are a rider. Now stop riding in the wrong car.

If God isn't the coach, I'm not on the team.

If you stop telling your "friends" all of your business, your enemies wouldn't know so much.

A person with nothing to lose will help you lose everything you have ever worked for.

You keep asking for peace, but can you handle the peace you seek?

Fear is a virus. Do not catch it.

The hardest thing that I have ever given was when I gave in.

ABOUT JENNIFER BISHOP

As an entrepreneur, author, faith-leader, influencer, motivational speaker, philanthropist, and a political & community activist, Jennifer is also a realist. She is a firm believer that the only way to make a difference is to be different than the status quo.

Taught early in her childhood the significance of education, Jennifer holds steadfast to the desire to learn and to pursue knowledge. Holding a Bachelor of Arts in History and a Master of Public Administration from Savannah State University, Jennifer is currently pursuing her Ph.D. in Organizational Leadership.

In 2008, while enjoying a long and successful career in business development within the senior leadership of Fortune 500 companies, Jennifer, like millions of others, was laid-off due to what became known as the Great Recession of 2008, all while expecting her son. At that moment, a decision had to be made that would determine the rest of her life. Would she lay down and fall into an emotional comma or stand and pursue what God promised her? The hard question had a simple answer. Jennifer told herself what she now tells others today, "Life knocking your down to the ground is not a punishment nor is it a crime. Staying down on the ground is. Now get up and go be great!"

Made in the USA
Columbia, SC
18 May 2022

60578454R00043